S0-CAA-984

A Few
Thoughts on Trout

A Few Thoughts on Trout

By Harold Cole
Illustrated by Betty Christensen

JULIAN MESSNER Ⓜ NEW YORK

A DIVISION OF SIMON & SCHUSTER, INC.

Copyright © 1986 by Harold Cole. All rights reserved including the right of reproduction in whole or in part in any form. Published by Julian Messner, A Division of Simon & Schuster, Inc. Simon & Schuster Building, Rockefeller Center, 1230 Avenue of the Americas, New York, New York 10020. JULIAN MESSNER and colophon are trademarks of Simon & Schuster, Inc. Manufactured in the United States of America

10   9   8   7   6   5   4   3   2   1

Library of Congress Cataloguing in Publication Data

Cole, Harold. A Few Thoughts on Trout. Summary: A young fisher shows two greedy adults his secrets of catching trout in his favorite unspoiled brook, only to regret it when they abuse the privilege. [1. Fishing — Fiction.   2. Conservation of natural resources — Fiction] I. Christensen, Betty, ill. II. Title. PZ7.C67344Fe 1985   [Fic]   85-30742 ISBN 0-671-60531-3 (lib. bdg.)

Dedicated To Frank and Marguerite Lundin

If all boys were as lucky as I was lucky to be taught to fish and have it served on the table then all boys would become fishermen.

Today there would be a little advantage. It was opening day of the fishing season. There were no other human tracks to be seen. I was the first.

Leaning ever more forward and trying to get even lower to the ground, I moved closer. My knee sank into the cold, damp earth.

In front of me lay the sand pool. It was the hardest to fish. There was no cover to hide me.

I swung the pole in a low sweeping motion. The seven or eight feet of line that I held against the pole were released at just the right time. The small red wriggling garden worm arched out and started to drop. It hit perfectly in the rushing water at the head of the pool.

Lowering the pole as much as possible and raising my head just a little, I watched the braided green line slide down through the middle of the pool. I had crossed the brook above the pool so my shadow wouldn't fall on the water and betray my presence.

Slowly, I began to raise the tip of the pole. It stopped. A heavy weight seemed hooked to the end. As I applied a little more pressure, I could feel the fish as it shook its head from one side to the other, trying to stabilize itself in the current.

With a sudden pull, the fish flew out of the pool over my right shoulder and lay flopping on the grass behind me. The twelve-inch brook trout had taken on the color of the sand pool.

I loosened the string that was around the burlap bag and slid the trout in with the others. It was a lighter color than the rest.

Two more, and I would have my limit.

The next pool was easy. The brook narrowed down and ran between nine or ten large clumps of grass. The grass on each knob streamed in the water. It was one of the deeper spots in the brook, and very black. The trout had the worm before it got to the second bog of grass, and I flipped it up on the bank. This one was jet black. Its red-and-orange belly with a gray-and-white stripe down the middle looked even darker as I slid it into the bag next to the fish from the sand pool.

The sun was coming up now and, although it felt good, the bright light on the water would make the fish harder to catch. I moved along, skipping some of the smaller pools, until I came to the bend in the brook.

The deep hole under the old stump looked better than ever. Barbed wire crossed several feet above the stump; it separated the field from the woods.

Leaning over the fence a little, I dropped my worm next to the stump. As soon as the worm disappeared into the inky blackness, the pole was yanked down almost out of my hands. With a great heave, I pulled the fish from the water.

The motion was quick and smooth. But, as the fish cleared the water, the hook slipped. I had pulled the fish up, but also sideways, and now it lay flopping on the bank a foot or so from the water.

Dropping the pole, I jumped over the fence. I felt the jab of the top strands of barbed wire, and a small pain, as skin and pants gave way to my effort to catch the fish.

Springing loose from the wire, I pounced on the fish just as it started to slide down the bank. My fingers quickly found its gills. Only then was it mine. It was huge—probably fourteen inches long—very large for this brook, which was my favorite.

Sitting down, I took the trout out of the burlap bag one by one. There were ten. Some were eight inches long, but they were mostly ten or eleven. A couple were twelve inches, and the largest was the one I had just caught.

Digging a hole by the brook, I cleaned my fish, putting the innards in the hole and covering them up. After washing the fish, I put them all back into the bag. It was heavy now. It felt good hanging from my belt.

I headed down the brook. I had wound my line around the end of the pole. It was a good pole. My father had gone out the night before and cut it for me. It was made of hickory. My father knew all the kinds of wood and what each was best for—he just did not like fishing.

When I hit the tar road, I hid my pole and headed down to the river. When I got to Stony Hole, I sat down on the bank to watch the men fish. Some had great high boots and long slender poles with reels that held the line. They did not have to wrap the line around the end of the pole like I did. They were fishing for brown trout, or at least that is what they called them. I had seen some. They looked more yellow than brown to me, and they had large red spots, probably from the liver everyone said they were fed. I had always heard they were not very good eating, but still everyone seemed to keep them.

As I sat there in the sun, my pants started to dry. The dark mud seemed to turn light, and soon I would be able to brush it off. I stuck my finger through the hole in the bottom of my sneaker and rubbed the bruise made by the sticks and stones that had found their way inside.

Noticing the rip in my pants for the first time, I remembered the fence where I had caught the big one. Pulling my pants up, I was surprised to see the blood had run all the way down my leg. It was dry and dark red now, and orange where it ran into the mud on my legs.

"Here he comes," someone said.

Everyone was looking downstream. I quickly pulled my pants leg back down, and as I looked I could see a man dressed in green. A shiver ran through me. Slowly he worked his way upstream. He would look at a man's license first, then in his fish creel, and then go on to the next man. He was the game warden.

Too many times my father had said, "If you take more than your limit, the game warden will put you in jail."

A fear started to creep over me. What if I had counted wrong? It was too late to run. I moved up a little closer to the tree, partly covering my bag of fish with my leg. As the warden worked his way upstream, I noticed his hat. It was darker green than his shirt, and had a hard black visor in the front. I was reminded of the uniform on an enemy general I had recently seen on a war poster.

He was not as big as I thought a warden would be. He almost seemed like a regular-size man. He finally walked up to me; however, he did not stop.

As he went by he said, "Any luck, son?"

I did not answer, and soon he was upstream, out of sight.

After a while, a man came up the bank of the river and sat down next to me.

"Why aren't you fishing?" he asked.

"I got my limit," I said.

The man grinned.

"How many is your limit?" he asked.

I said, "Ten," but I could see he did not believe me.

I really did not care.

"Why don't you show me?" he said.

I did not see anything wrong with showing him, so I untied my bag. The first one I pulled out was the 14-incher. I thought his eyes would pop out. Slowly, I pulled out all ten. This time I lined them up—largest one first, down to the smallest. The man just kept staring at my fish as if he had never seen any like them.

After a while he said, "I will give you ten dollars for them."

"You do not sell fish or game," I said, "you eat it. This is supper for me and my brothers and sisters."

"I was only kidding," the man said.

I knew he was lying.

I reached down to put my fish back in the bag when the man said, "Wait a minute. I want a friend of mine to see them. Hey, Joe," he hollered to a man out in the stream. "Come over here."

The man named Joe came out of the river. His friend pointed down at my fish.

"Wow! look at that," he said. "Where did you catch them?"

"In a secret place," I answered. "No one goes there but me."

"Is it a private pond?" he asked.

"No," I said.

I could see he did not know much about trout. Whoever heard of catching one in a pond? I bet he is from the city, I thought to myself. He has never seen the brooks that tumble down through the woods, gurgling as if they were singing and trying to find their way to the ocean. This is where the native brook trout lived, not in the river. The only trout he knew were the ones the truck had put in the river two days earlier so the city fishermen could catch something.

The two men looked at each other for a minute, then one of them asked, "Have you had breakfast yet?"

"Yah, a long time ago," I said.

The thought came into my mind of the sandwich my mother had made for me the night before. She had fried an egg and asked if two pieces of heel bread would be all right.

"Sure," I said, thinking of someone who probably had none at all.

I had sat by the brook waiting for daylight and thought, "Why carry the sandwich when I can eat it now and not waste time later?"

I had rolled up the onion bag that I carried the sandwich in and stuffed it in my pocket. I would need it later, on the way back. I would pick up soda bottles along the road. Maybe today I would find a quart Coca-Cola bottle or a Diamond Ginger Ale. They were worth five cents each. There were always two-cent ones to be found. If I was lucky I could get a soda and maybe cupcakes, and if I was really lucky, a candy bar. There were always ways. So what if I did not have any money like some of the other boys, and anyway, they did not know how to catch trout.

"Well, do you want to go for breakfast with us?" one of the men asked again.

It was eleven o'clock. I was not hungry—I was starving to death. Even the thought of food made my stomach hurt.

"What kind of breakfast?" I asked.

"Oh, how about ham and eggs?" one of them said.

Ham and eggs, I thought.

I remembered a long time before, we had raised a pig and butchered it. A friend of my father's had smoked the ham and the bacon.

It had been great; however, I had never been to a restaurant.

"Why do you want to take me for breakfast?" I asked.

"Well," one of them said, "the fish here are not biting, and after we go and fish in the brook where you got yours we will go for breakfast."

"No," I said, "my mother would not like me to go with strangers and, furthermore, I only fish my brook three times a year so there will always be some left. I would never fish it twice in one day."

"Well, do you know any others?" the one called Joe asked.

"Oh, sure, lots," I said.

"How about if we have breakfast first," Joe said, "then we will go fishing with you."

"Do you have any worms?" I asked.

"Just night crawlers," one said.

"They won't work," I said, "you've got to have worms and small hooks."

I remembered Willie Aquilar, who worked at Canfield's Drug Store. I had gone up the night before. I had saved my money for a long time for the opening day of fishing season. I had stood at the showcase. When old Harry Canfield asked if he could help me I said, "No, I am just looking."

I knew him. He would not give me any kind of break. I think he knew I was waiting for Willie. Finally he went away and Willie came over. I showed him my thirty-four cents.

"What do you need?" he asked.

"Fish lines and hooks," I answered.

I could already see the braided green line. It came in hanks, one tied to another. My heart sank as I read the price. Fifty cents.

"Let's see," said Willie. "These two are hooked together. They must be twenty-five cents each."

I knew they had been thirty cents for one hank.

All the lines on the spool were a dollar or more. Willie quickly cut one off, taking the price tag off and tying it on the next hank.

"What kind of hooks?" he asked.

"Just little ones. The kind you use for brook trout," I said.

"How many do you want?" he asked.

"Well, nine cents' worth," I said.

I knew they were one cent each. I also knew Willie would give me several extra. Willie got the box down and opened the lid. There were many compartments with different sizes in each one. I started to pick out the small hooks, one at a time. Nine would have to be enough.

When I got the pile finished, Willie said, "Them are awful small. I think you better take two for a penny."

I grinned. Willie reached in and grabbed nine more and quickly stuffed them into a small bag. Taking my thirty-four cents, Willie counted the change.

"Let's see," he said, "twenty-five cents for line, four cents for hooks. It looks to me like you got enough left for a five-cent ice cream cone."

The grin must have shown on my face. As I looked up, old Harry was watching from behind the counter. I think he knew why I wanted Willie to wait on me, but he said nothing.

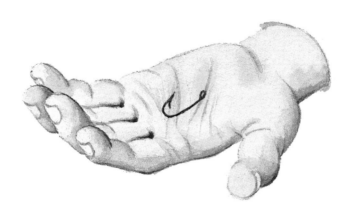

"We don't have any small hooks," one of the city fishermen said.

Although I had already decided not to take them fishing, I could almost smell the ham cooking.

"Well, let's go to breakfast first," Joe said.

I don't even remember deciding to go, but I did and the breakfast was good. Ham, eggs, toast, and chocolate milk. Some people walked by from town.

I felt big sitting next to the two fishermen. They had left their high boots on, and they really did look like giant green frogs.

One by one I thought of brooks to take them to, but each time I would remember one of my favorite holes I would discard the choice. I wondered if I had taken them fishing first, would they have taken me to breakfast afterwards? I thought of my father. He always said a man was only as good as his word. I had said I would take them fishing, so I would.

After breakfast we went in their car. First we
went to where I had left my pole and worms. They
looked at my hickory pole sort of funny, but I said nothing.
For a moment I dangled my pole in the brook as if I were fishing. I
wished now I had released more trout in the morning, so I could still
fish. I had decided on a brook that ran between two roads. It was
heavy with brush, but it always had good big fish in it. I don't think
they knew the seven-to-nine inchers were the best eating.

They went crashing down through the brush. I knew they were
making too much noise. They said my hooks were too small and they
would use their bigger ones. They also wanted to use their night
crawlers. They kept saying they only wanted the big ones. I walked
along behind them. After a while they started to get mad.

One said, "There are no trout in this brook. You lied to us."

"No," I said, "I don't lie."

As I stood looking downstream, I saw a little mud washing along the current. As I looked, I realized it came from under a small flat rock a little way from shore.

I said, "There is one in this pool, but you already scared it. If you want it I will catch it for you."

"Go ahead," one of them said and started to pass me his pole.

"I won't need that," I said.

I moved down the pool until I got to the rock and, lying down, I slowly reached out past the rock, bringing my hand down around its back side. As my fingertips curled under the rock, I felt the trout. With a sudden movement, I forced it up against the rock and ran my fingers through its gills. In another quick movement I threw the eleven-inch brook trout out on the bank. Both men looked surprised. One picked it up and put it in his creel.

I quietly said, "Now if you will listen, I will show you how to catch trout. First, take those big hooks off and put mine on, then put one of my small worms on and stay behind me. You will have to be quiet."

Slowly, I moved downstream, and soon I located a good pool. I motioned one of them forward half-way toward me. I made him get down on his knees. When he reached me, I showed him the run of water that would carry his worm to the pool below.

"Try to get it to go under that big rock," I said.

The fish hit before the worm ever got to the rock. The man began to reel in line.

"Just flip it up on the bank," I said.

From then on they listened. As we went along, they spooked two
more and I caught them with my hands. By the time we got to the next
road, they each had four. Luckily the land across the road was posted.
 "How about upstream from the car?" one asked.
 "The brook is too small," I said.
 They let me off down by the river where they had picked me up.
I was happy I had helped them get some fish.

Little did I know what I had done. I would not know until Monday. On the way to school the bus went by my brook. I was shocked to see the green car I had taken there the first day of fishing.

"Oh well," I thought, "they just want to try it by themselves."

I gave it no more thought. The next morning on the way to school there were two cars. The green one was one of them.

That night after school I went to the brook. Both banks were trampled to mud. The limbs that overhung the brook were bent back. No more would the small bugs and caterpillars crawl out and fall into the brook and feed the trout. I crossed the road and went up into the woods. They had been there too. No fish darted around in the pool as I approached.

The brook was dead, and I had killed it.

Never again would I show any man my secret places. The men came back for several years and then they stopped. It was seven years before the brook got back to normal. For three years after the men stopped, I released every fish I caught in the brook. I grew into manhood before I caught an eleven-incher out of that brook.

It was too much to pay for ham and eggs.